The Miracle of the Human Body

Anatomy & Physiology for Children

Children's Anatomy & Physiology Books

Our body is one brilliant
machine with all parts
equally important.

Read on and learn
more about our body!

The Skeletal System

Our skeleton is the internal framework of our body. Its main functions are: support, movement, protection, production of blood cells, storage of ions and endocrine regulation

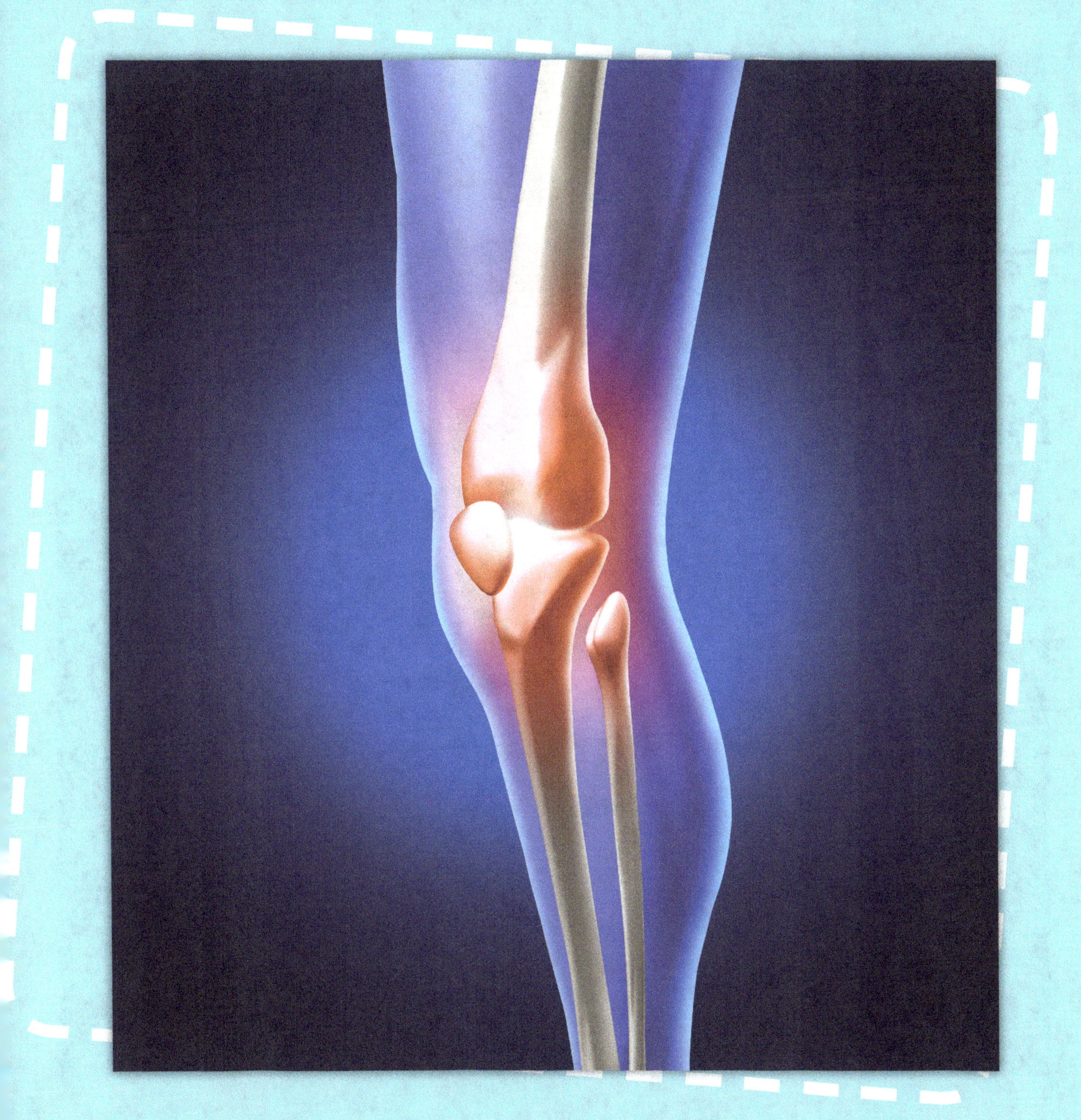

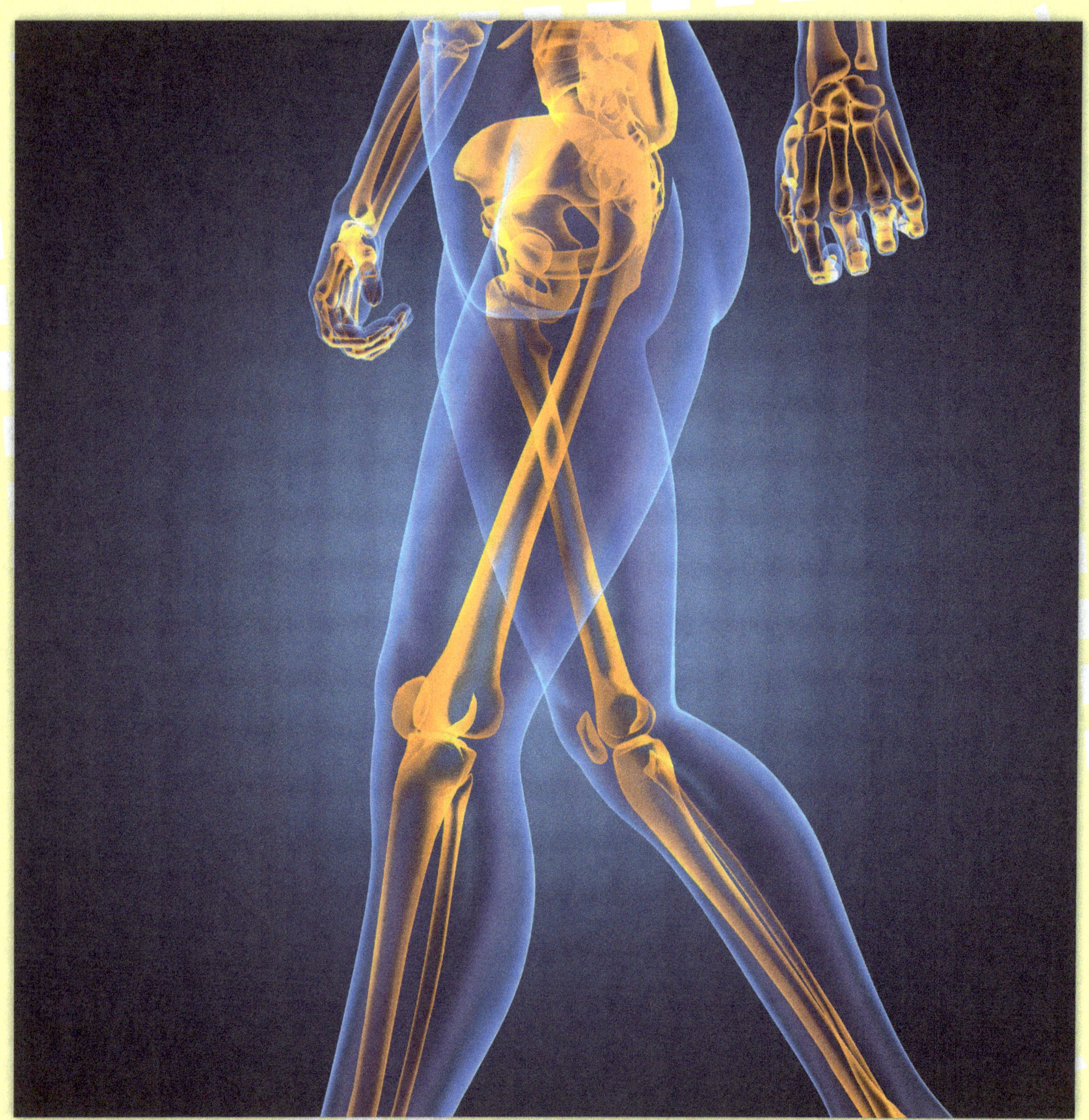

QUICK FACT:

We have 270 bones at birth, however it decreases to 206 bones since some bones have fused together as we grow old.

The Circulatory System

The circulatory system is the body system that allows blood to circulate and transport minerals and nutrients to and from cells in the body.

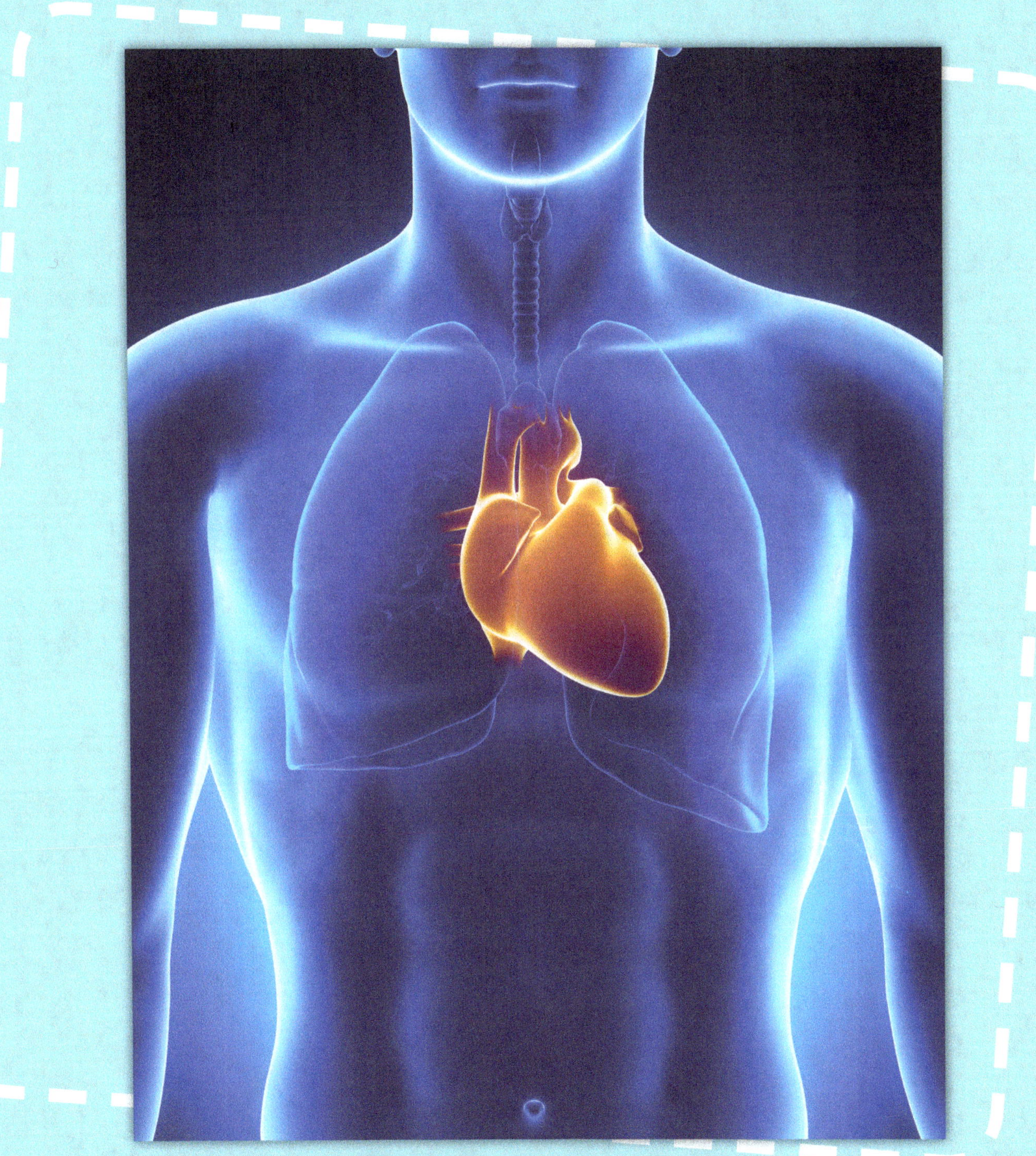

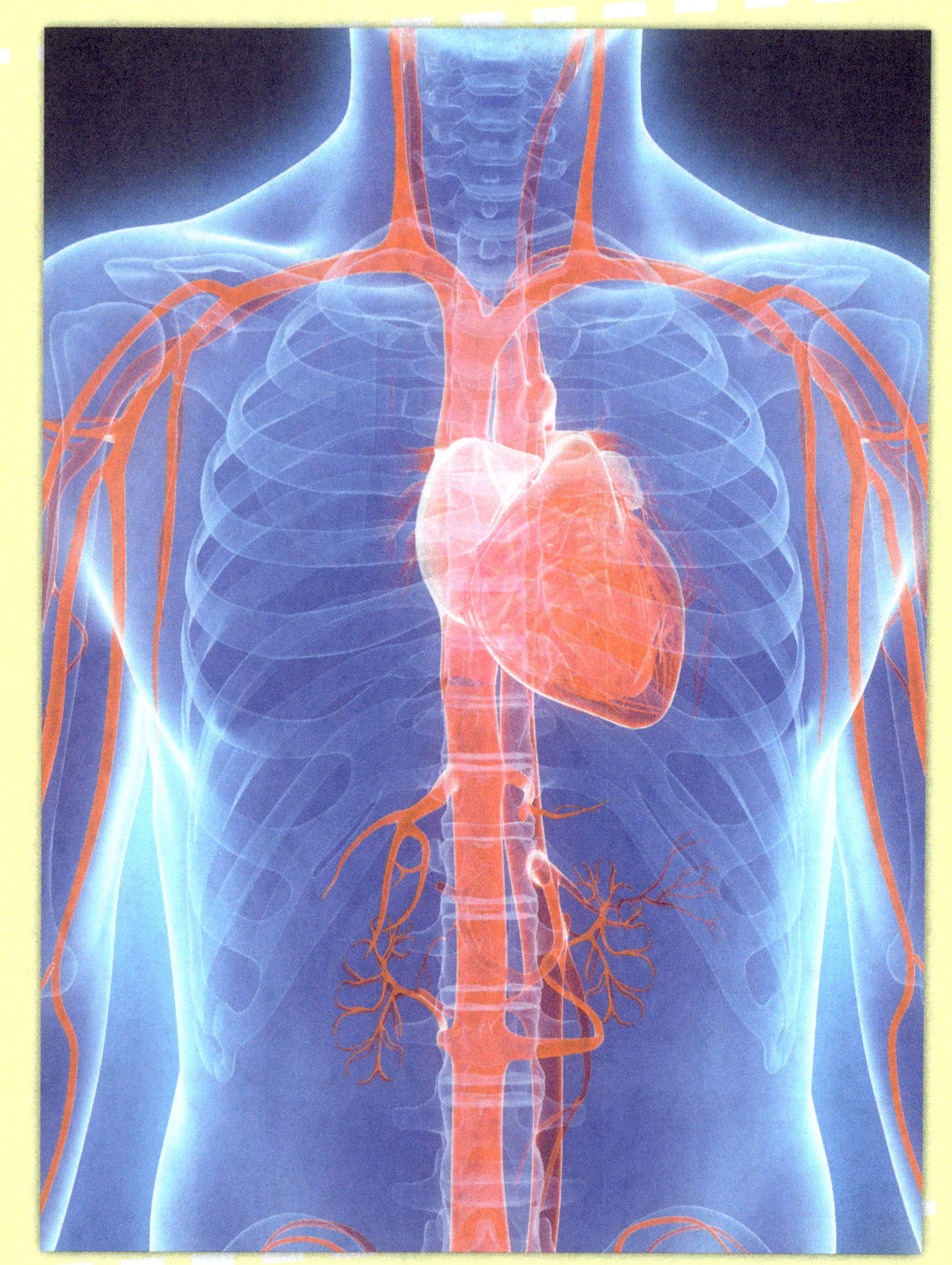

QUICK FACT:

Our circulatory system is really long! If you were to lay all veins in your body, it could wrap the planet around 2.5 times!

The Muscular System

This system consists of cardiac, smooth and skeletal muscles. It allows our body to move and maintain posture.

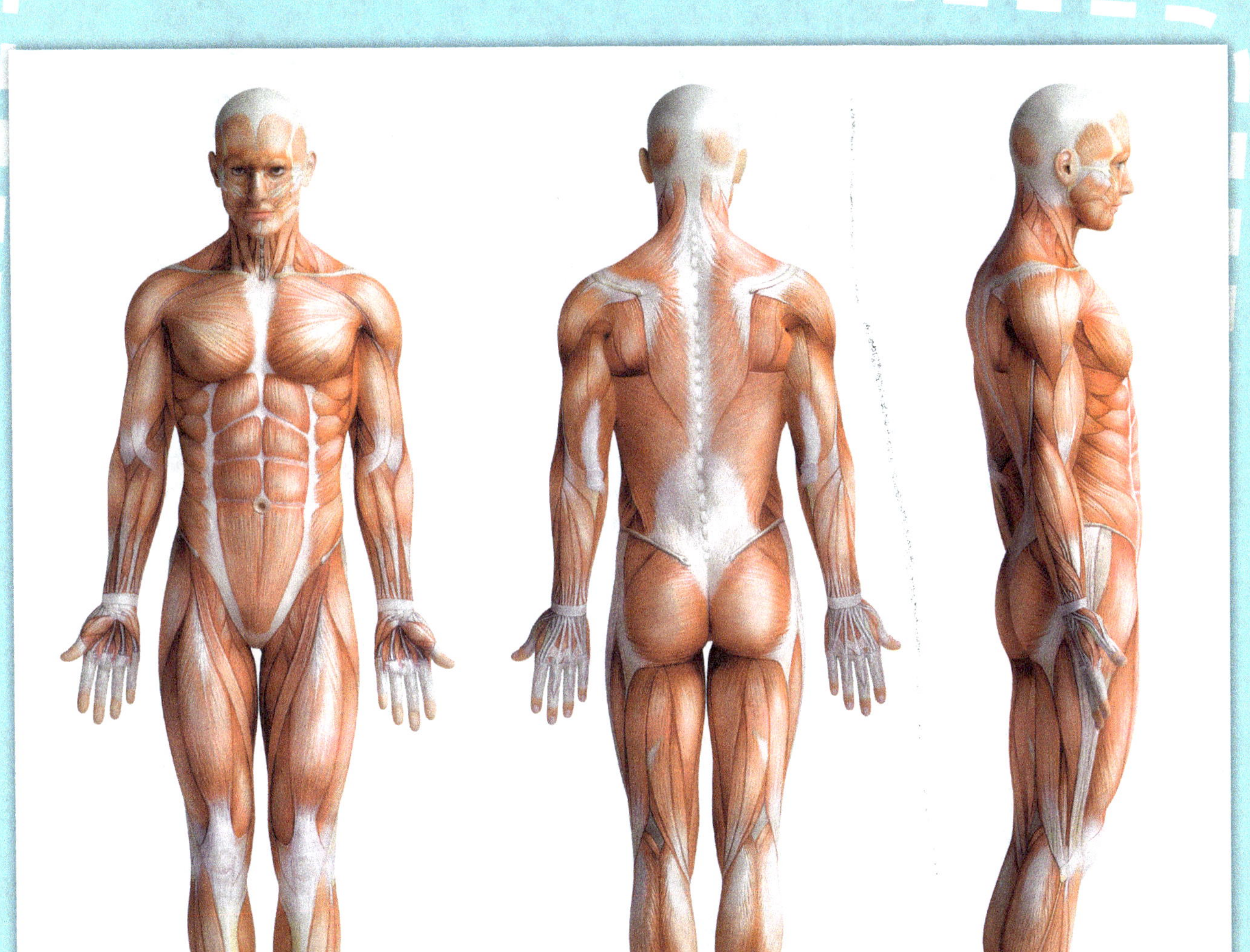

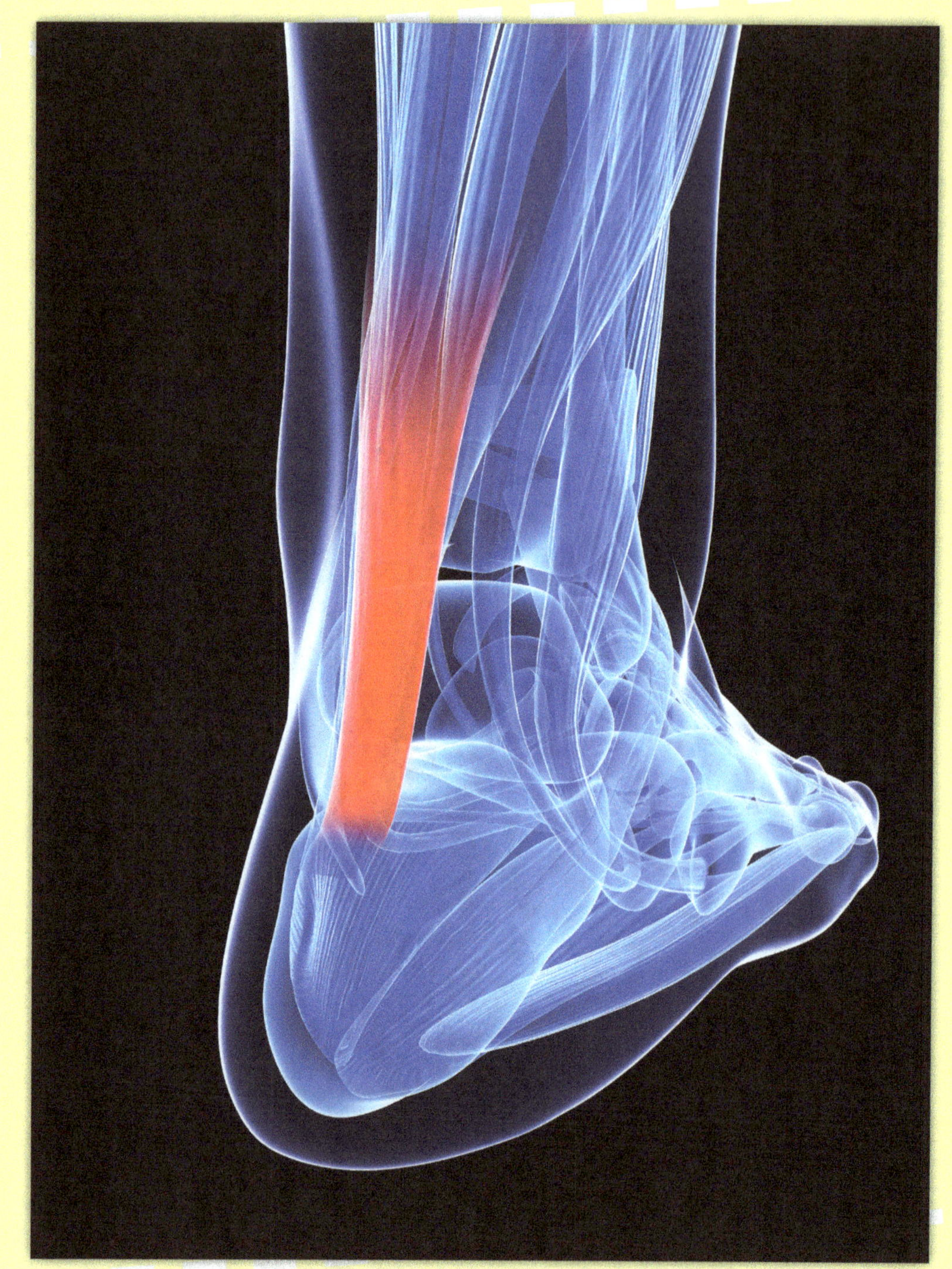

QUICK FACT:

The smallest muscle is in our ears. However, it is very important since it connects the ear and the ear drum together.

The Excretory System

This system removes excess and unnecessary materials from our body fluids like urine and sweat.

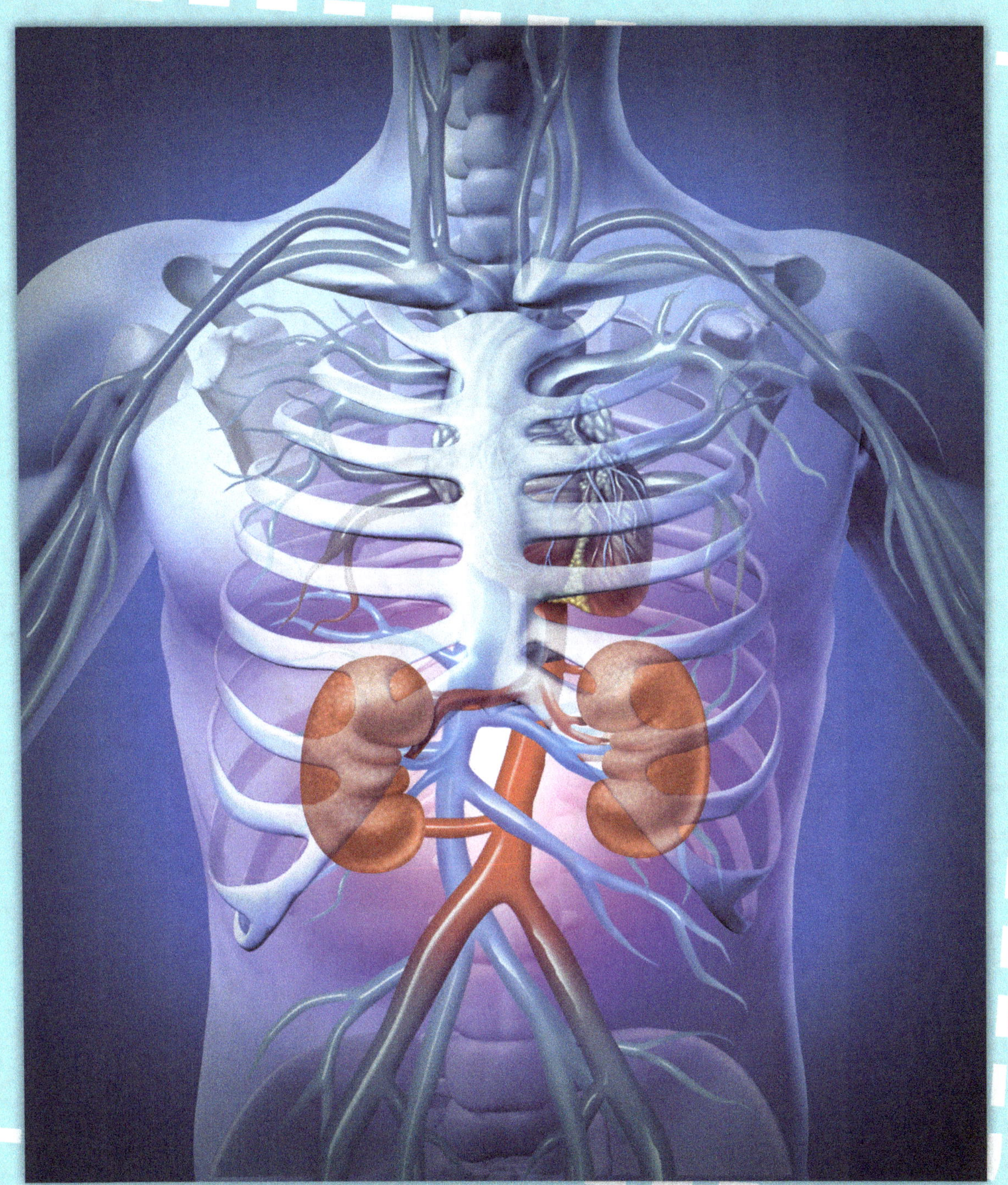

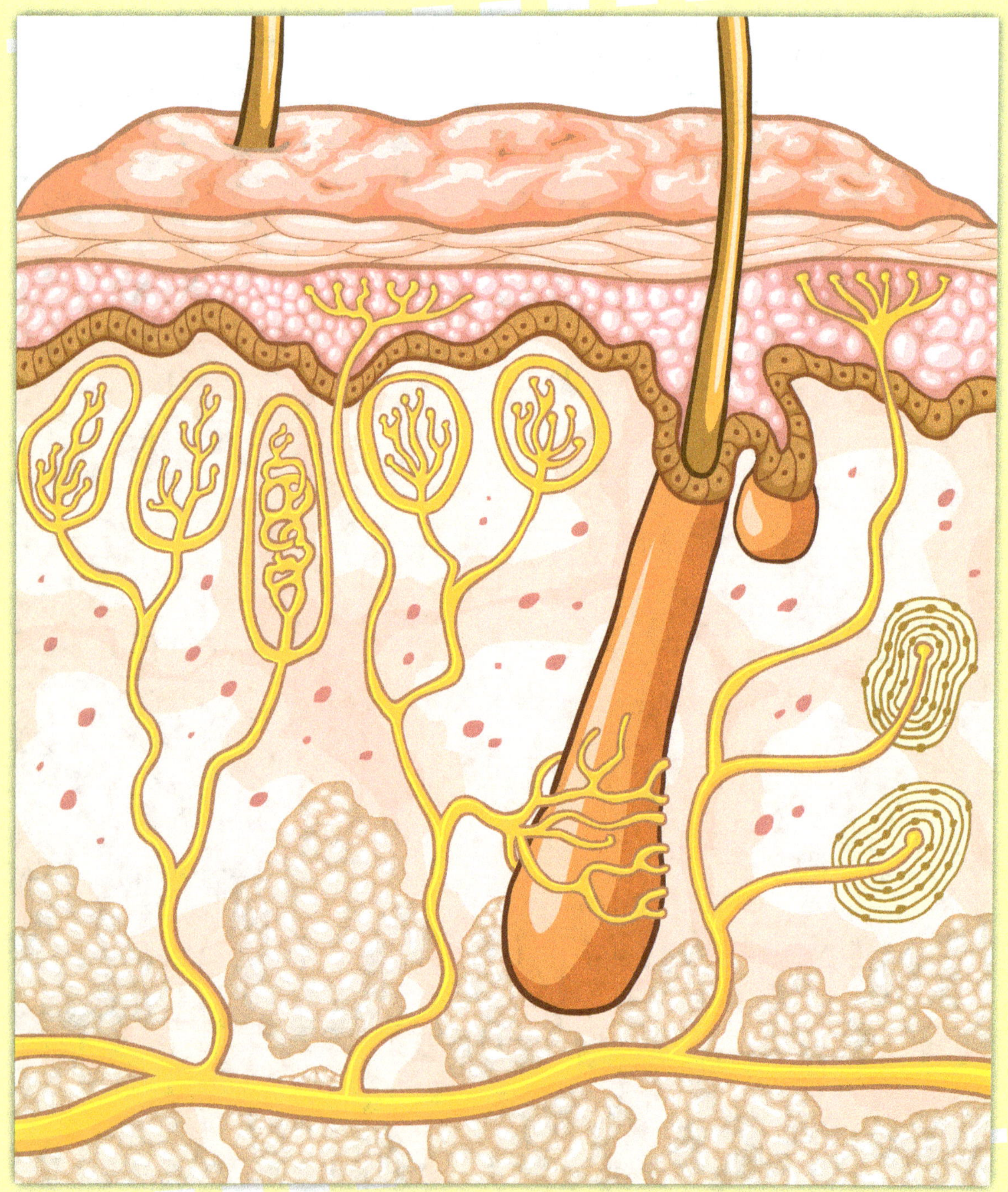

QUICK FACT:

The average number a person pees is 3000 times a year.

The Digestive System

The digestive system refers to the process of digestion. Its main function is to breakdown food into smaller components which can be absorbed into the body.

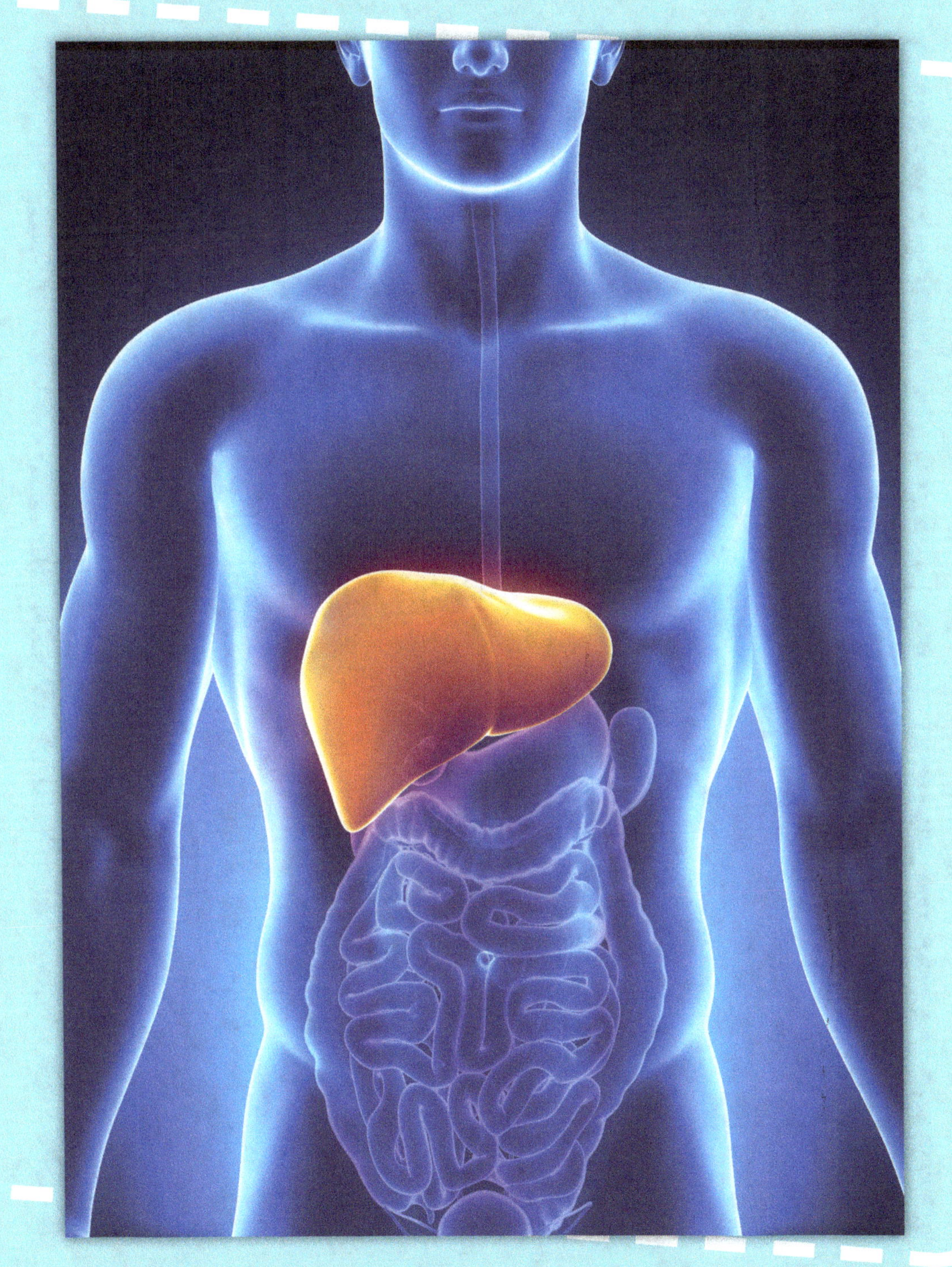

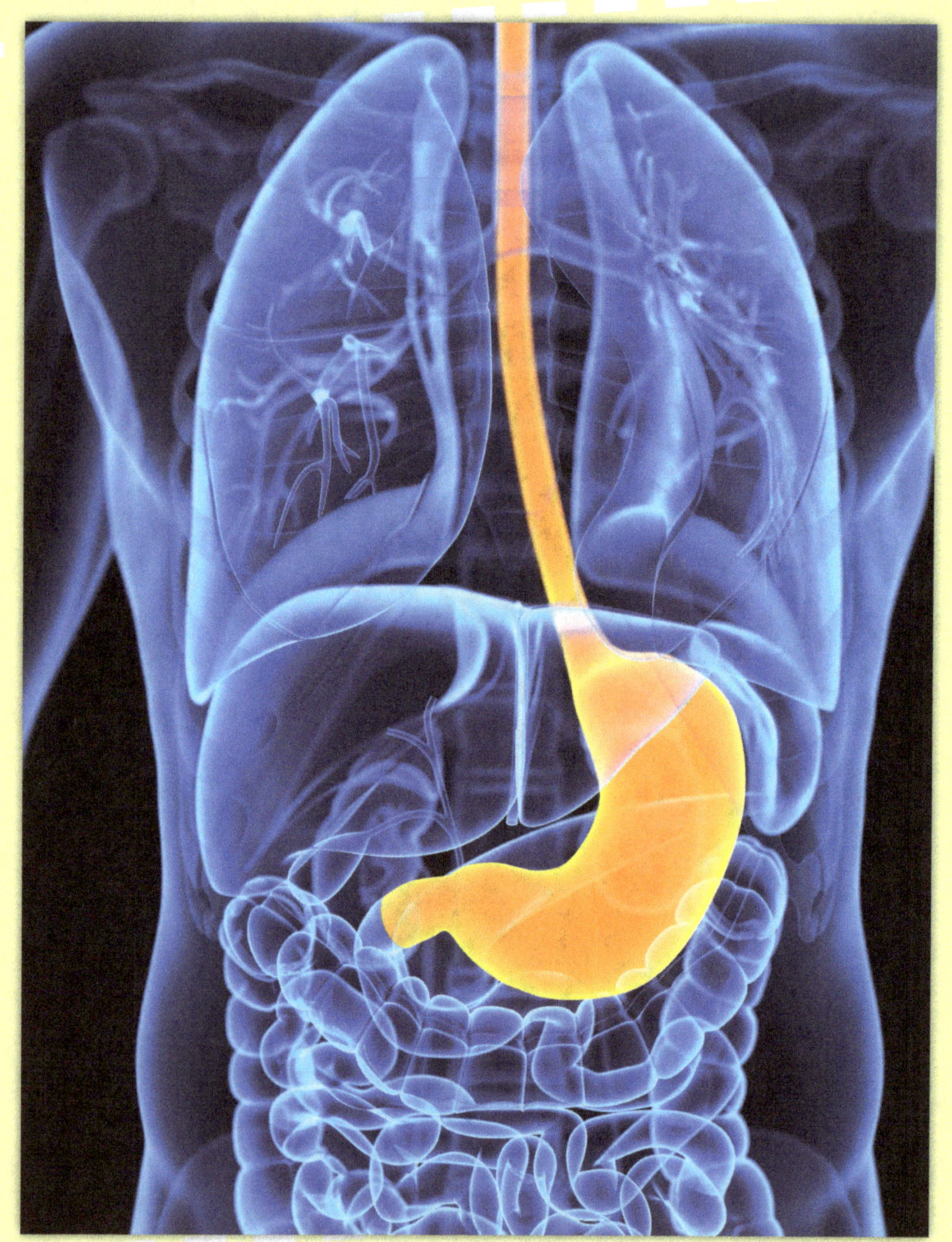

QUICK FACT:

This system is the most cancer-prone body system, much more than any other organ system in the body.

QUICK FACT:

There are about 400 different species of bacteria (good or bad) in our colon.

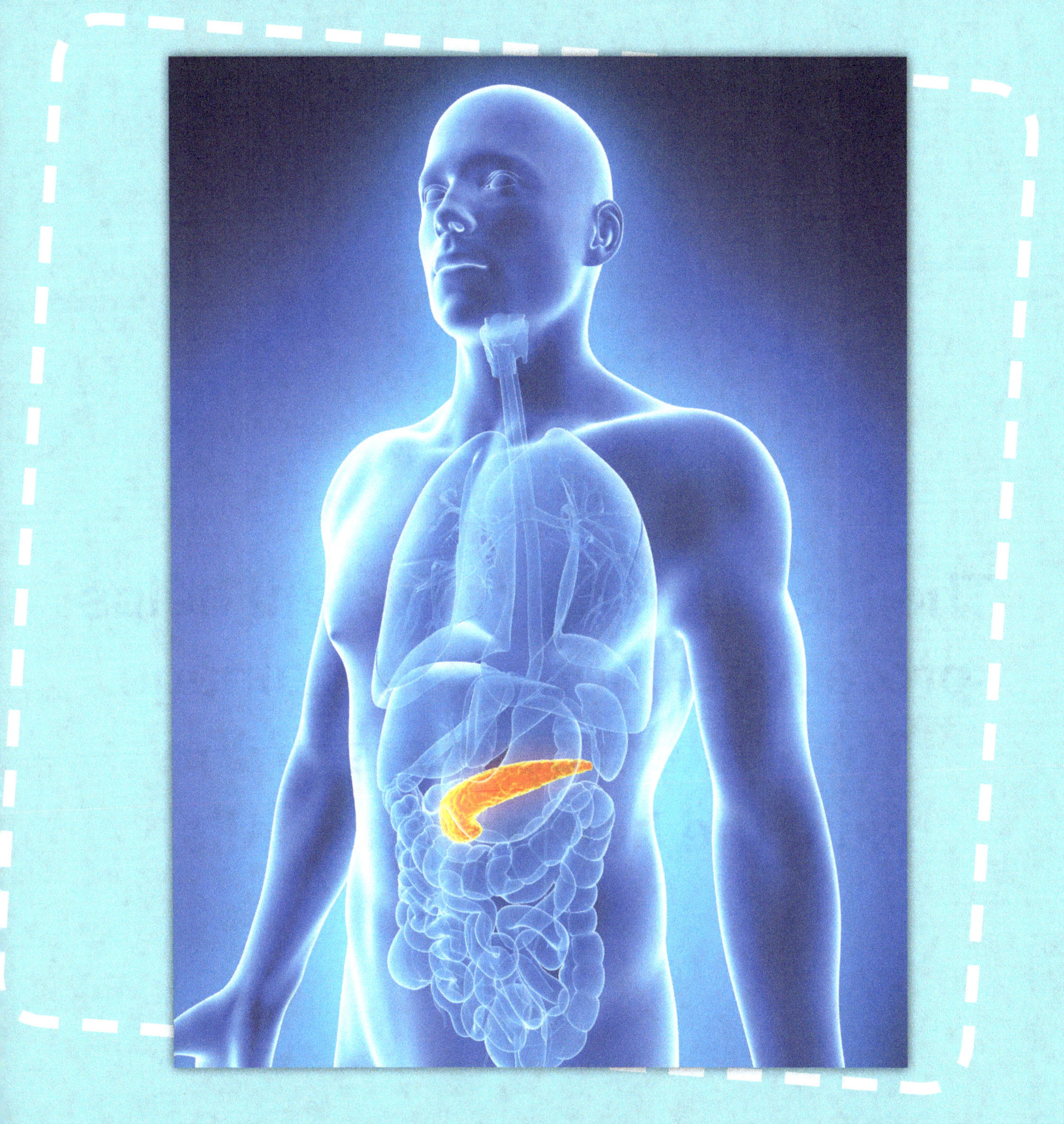

The Integumentary System

The Integumentary system helps protect our body from damage. The system consists of the skin, the hair and the nails.

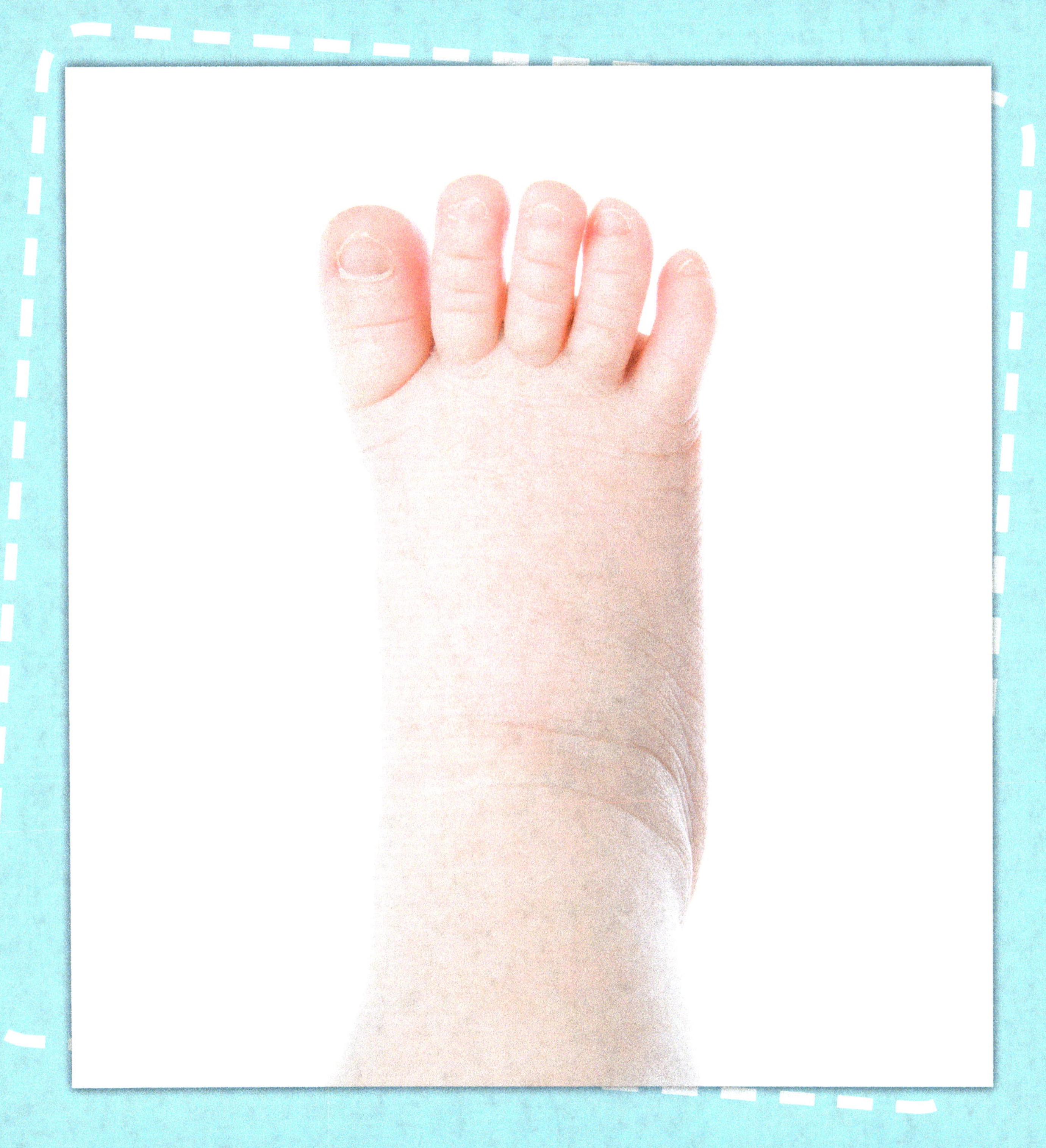

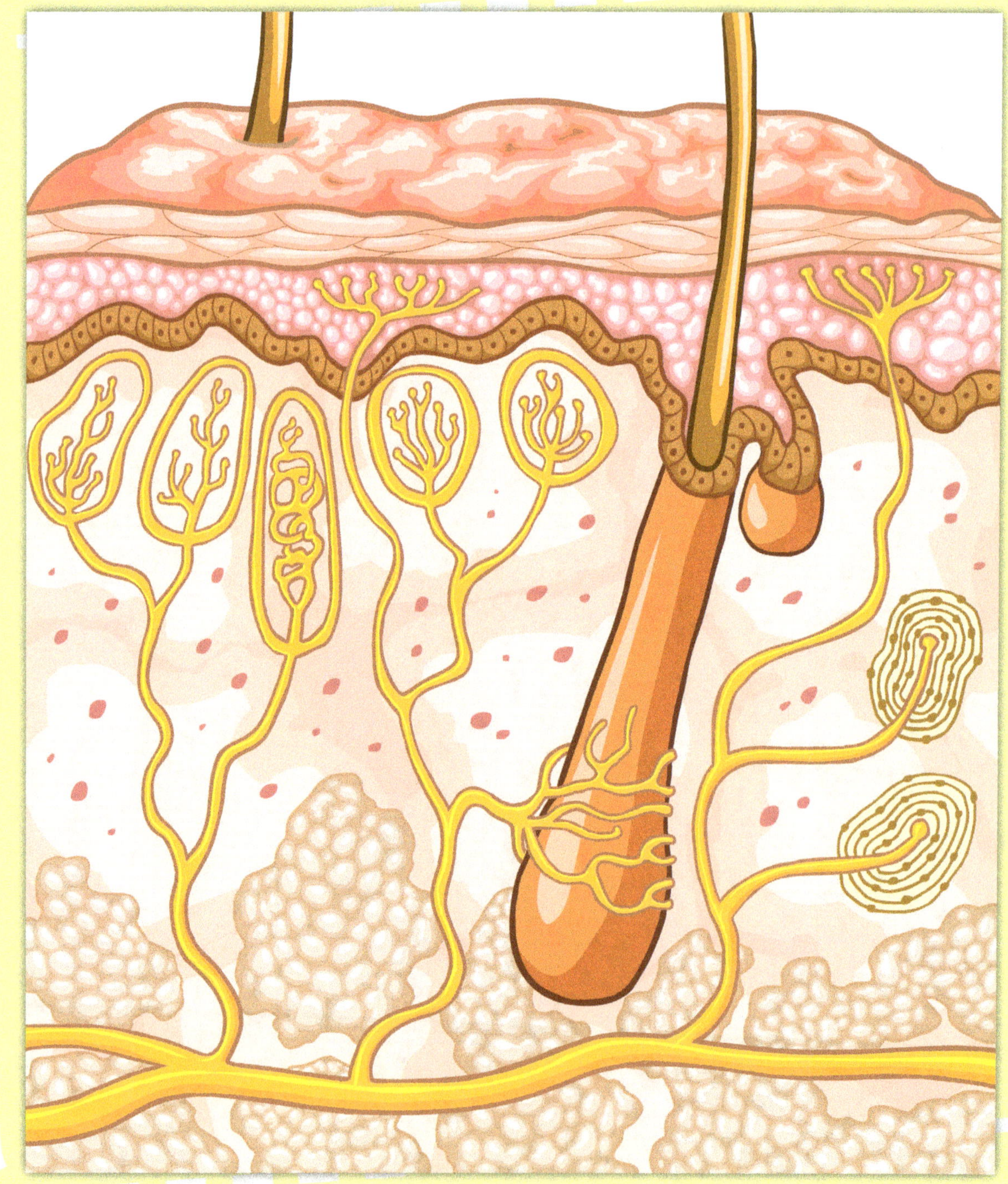

QUICK FACT:

We have a new layer of
skin every month.

The Nervous System

This system refers to the part of the body that coordinates its actions (voluntary and involuntary) and transmits signals between different parts of the body.

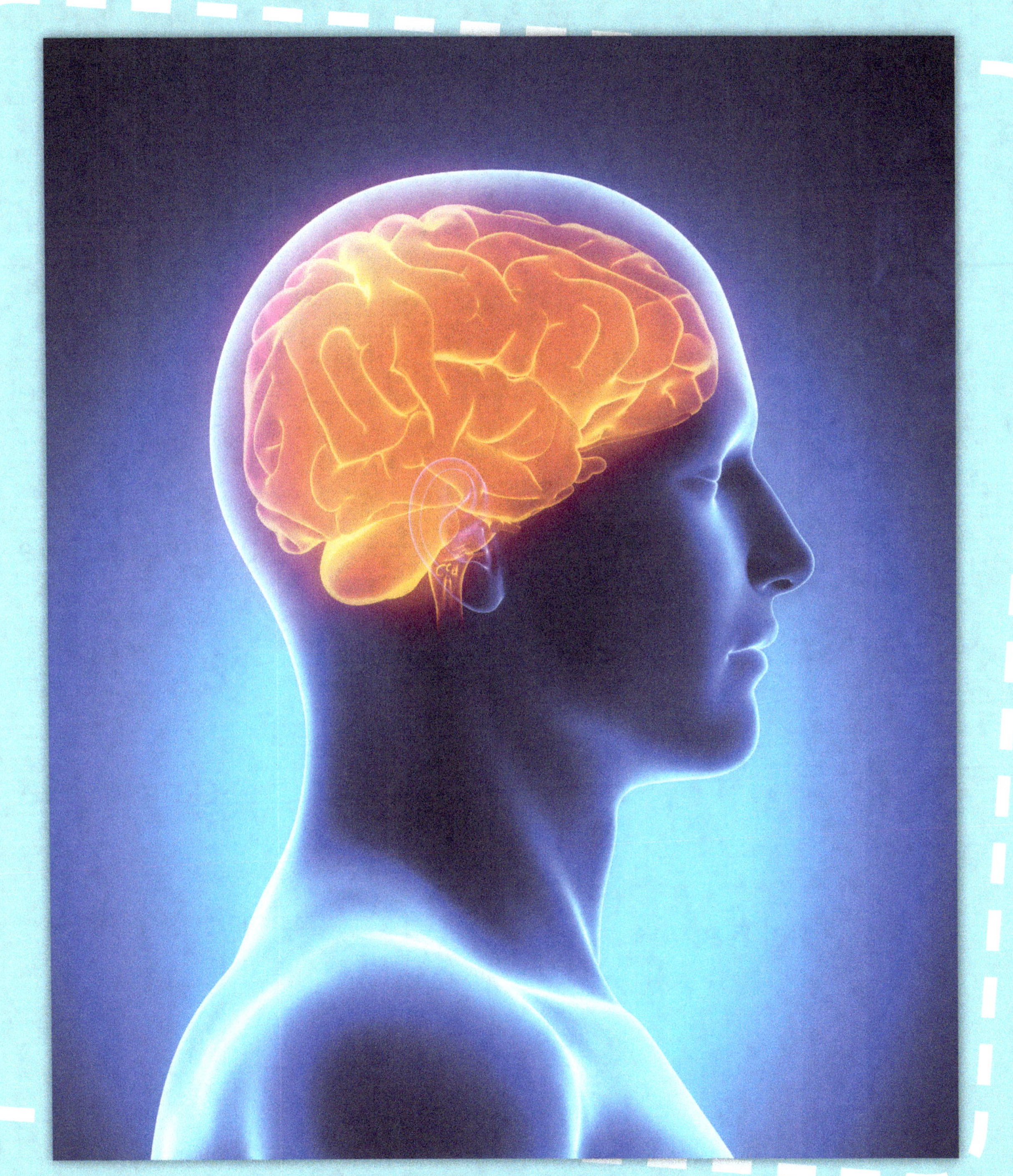

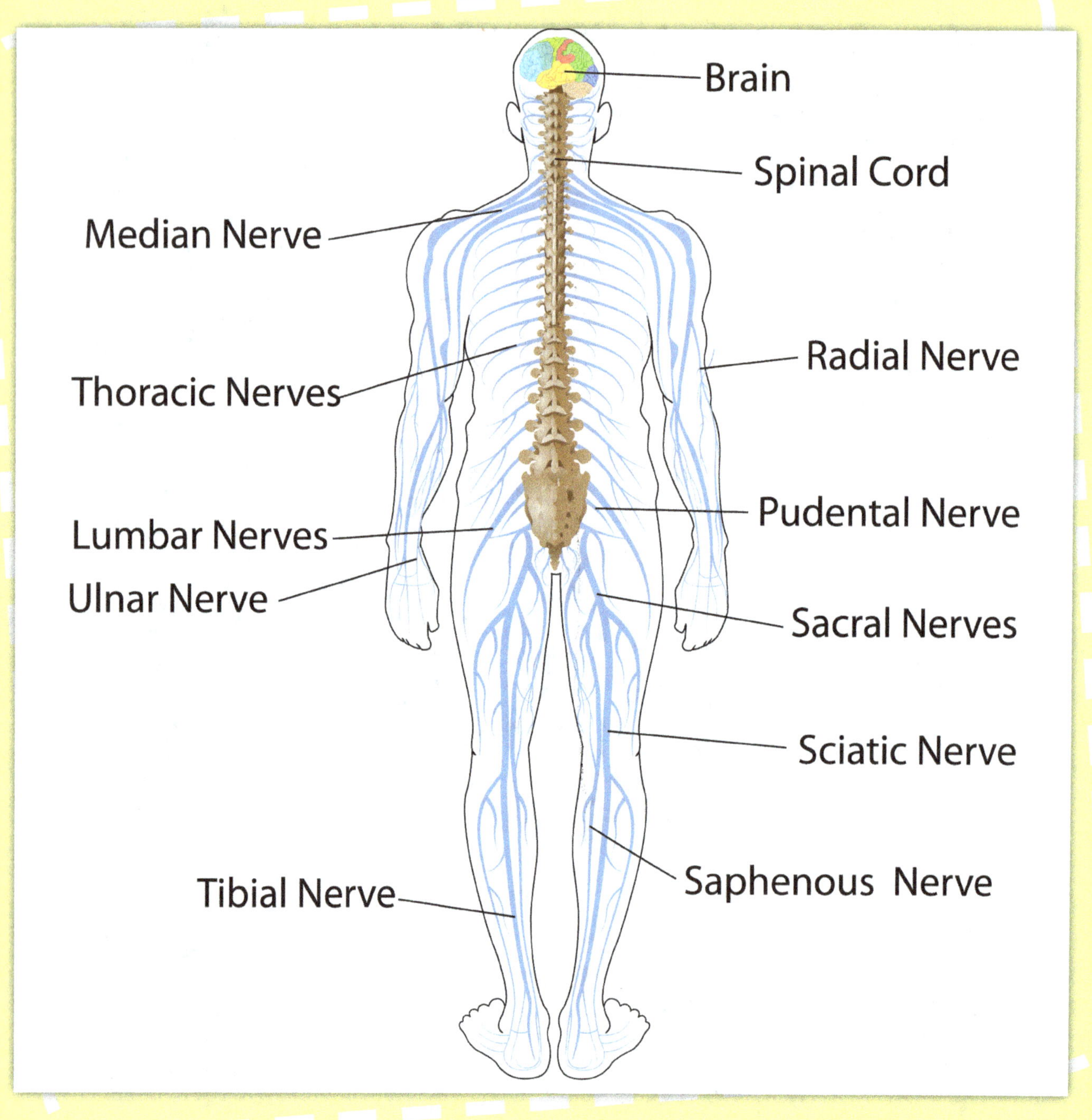

Brain
Spinal Cord
Median Nerve
Radial Nerve
Thoracic Nerves
Lumbar Nerves
Pudental Nerve
Ulnar Nerve
Sacral Nerves
Sciatic Nerve
Tibial Nerve
Saphenous Nerve

QUICK FACT:

As we grow older, our brain loses almost one gram per year.

The Endocrine System

The endocrine system is the collection of glands that secrete hormones directly to the circulatory system.

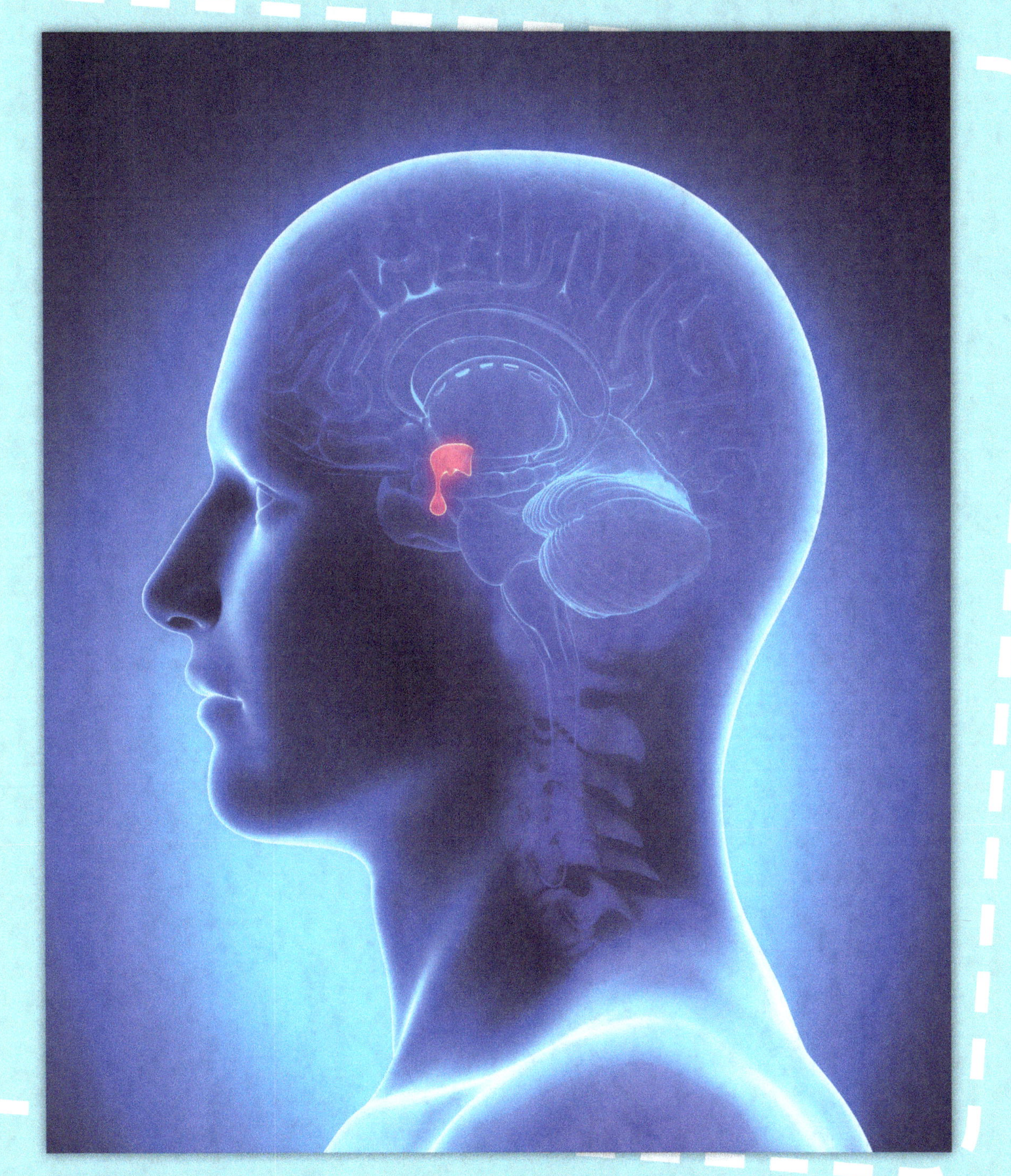

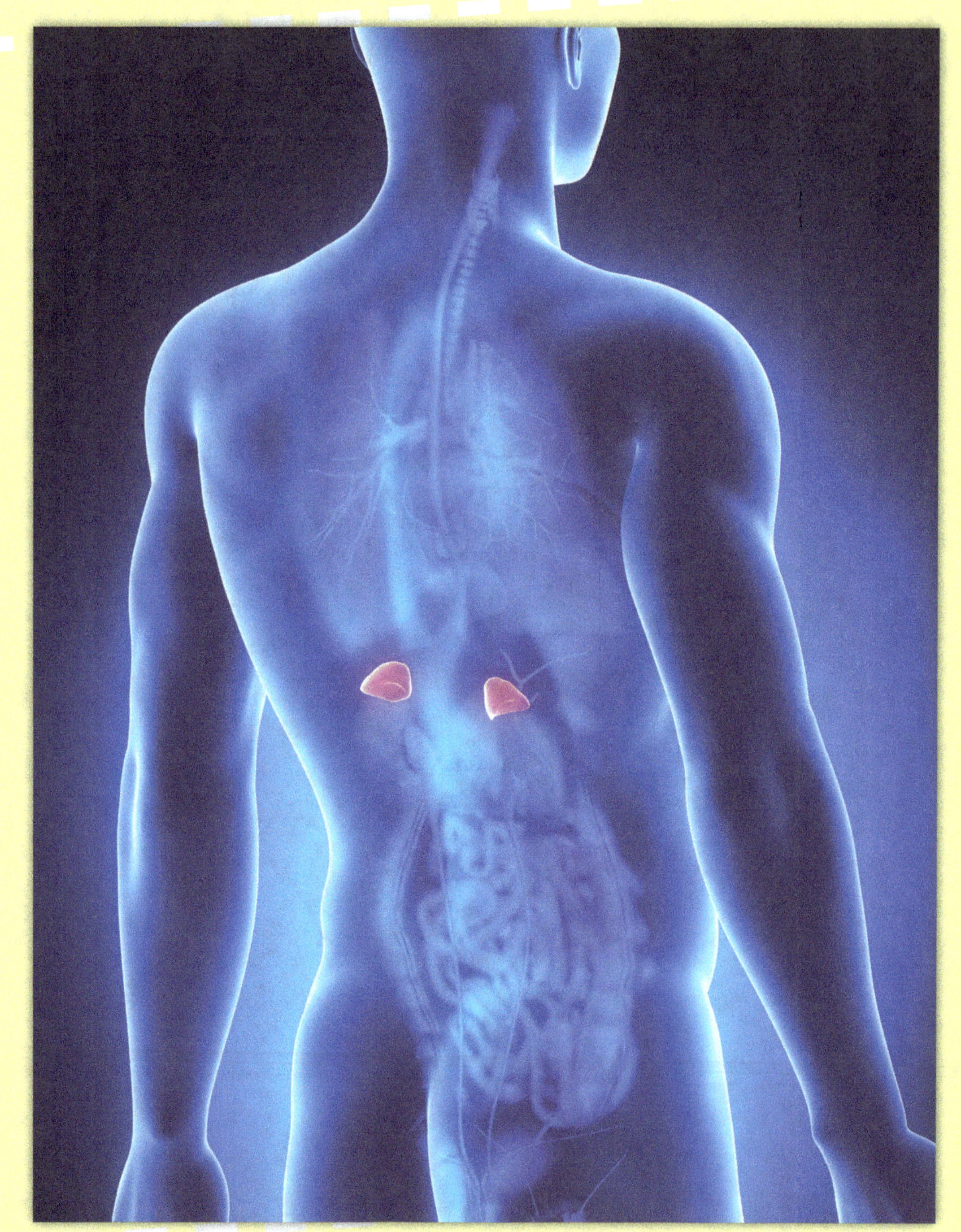

QUICK FACT:

The endocrine system helps us fight stress by secreting hormones to mobilize more energy.

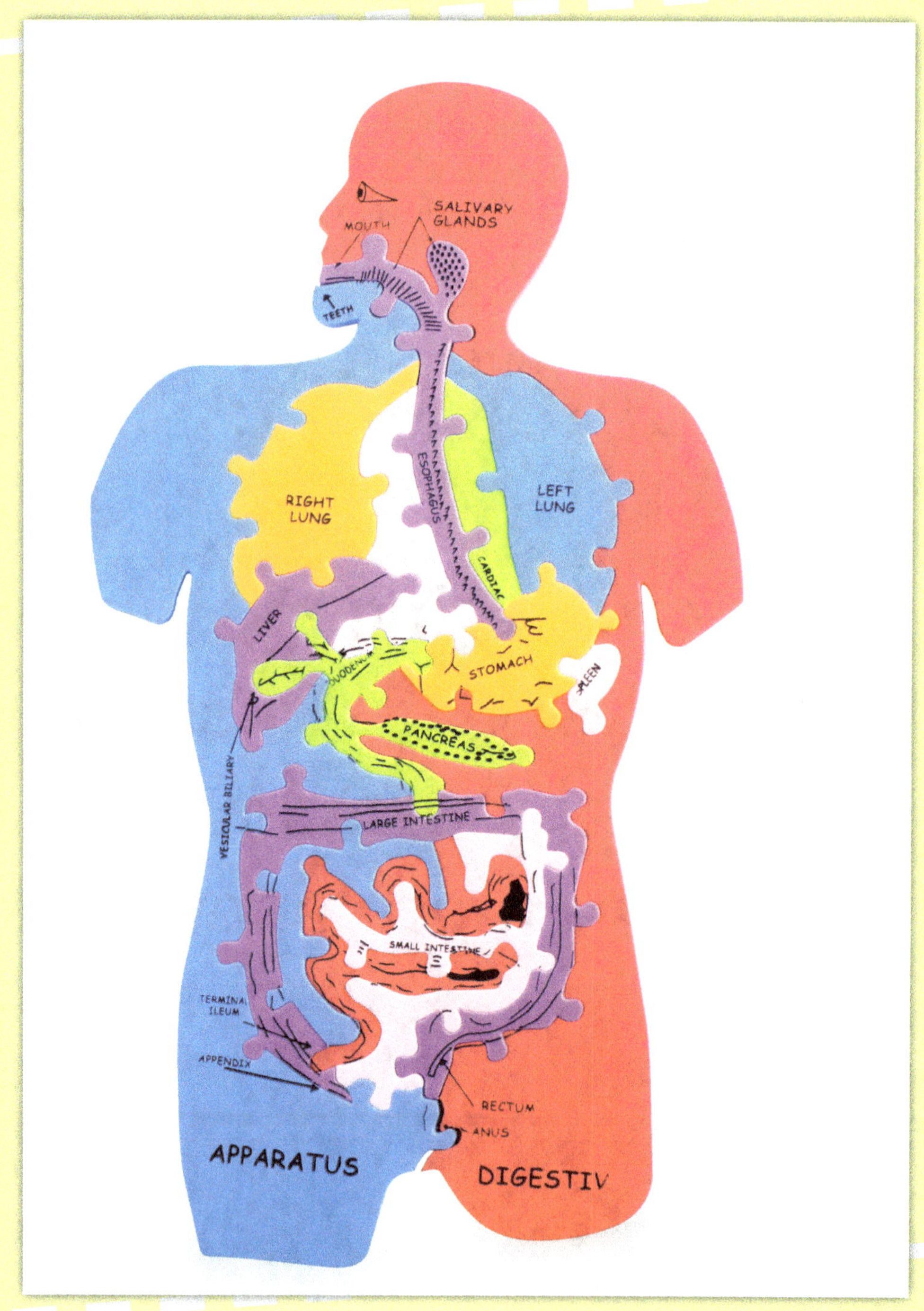

SALIVARY GLANDS
MOUTH
TEETH
RIGHT LUNG
LEFT LUNG
ESOPHAGUS
CARDIAC
LIVER
DUODENUM
STOMACH
SPLEEN
PANCREAS
VESICULAR BILIARY
LARGE INTESTINE
SMALL INTESTINE
TERMINAL ILEUM
APPENDIX
RECTUM
ANUS
APPARATUS
DIGESTIV

There is still a lot to learn about the human body.

Research and learn interesting facts! Have fun!

Visit
BABY PROFESSOR
EDUCATION KIDS
www.BabyProfessorBooks.com
to download Free Baby Professor eBooks
and view our catalog of new and exciting
Children's Books